The
European
Eel

The
European
Eel

Steve Ely

with artwork by
P.R. Ruby

Longbarrow Press

Published in 2021 by
Longbarrow Press
76 Holme Lane
Sheffield
S6 4JW

www.longbarrowpress.com

Printed by T.J. Books Ltd,
Padstow, Cornwall

ISBN 978-1-906175-41-2

First edition

Contents

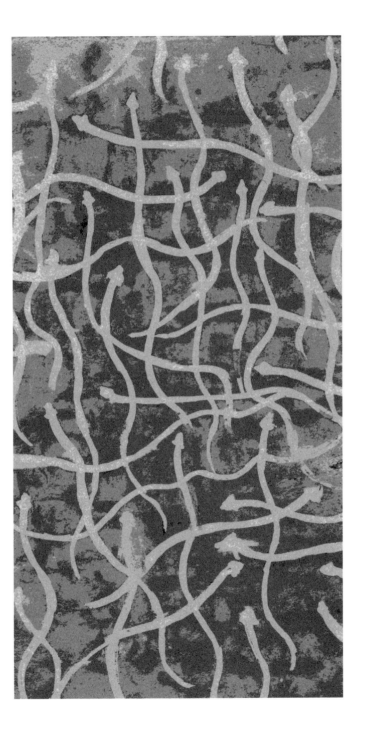

In the Subtropical Convergence Zone
of the southern Sargasso, over the edge of the Nares Abyssal,
south-east of the Bermuda Ridge, snow is rising
in the water column from fifteen hundred feet.
Somewhere in Tethys' salty darkness,
in spurts of milt and billowing roe, eels
are birthing their posterity, a spore-storm of eggs
in uncountable centillions, each buoyed
on its micron of oil. The embryos float
in the Miocene water like dust motes
caught in a shaft of light, and ascending
through the photocline, join the thermonuclear
microplankton of the drifting epipelagic.

In the eighteen-degree water, hatching,
it is hypothesised, takes place after two days
of embryonic growth, after which emerges
the pinhead imago—veined, elongate,
a leaf of transparent white willow—
leptocephalus, the larval form of anguilla,
absorbing its yolk-sac for ten or twelve days,
lengthening daily by micrometres,
gaining weight daily in microgrammes,
until a fortnight after hatching, the size
of a sand-grain or emphatic full-stop,
it unhinges its tiny, gaping jaws,
fangs half as long as its head, and hunts
in the eutrophic blizzard, seizing diatoms,
dinoflagellates, polyethylene microbeads,
fuelling-up for the thirty-month long haul,
Sargasso to the Biscay Abyssal.

Sargasso, a bright lens of brine sitting light
on the freeze of the Antarctic Bottoms,
herded to a hump by the North Atlantic Gyre.
The desert sea, life confined to its turbulent edges,
the highways of the eel, and the surface rafts
of drifting sargassum from which it takes its name.
The graveyard sea, swallower of troopships
and Grumman Avengers, where the drowned
float forever in zombied suspension
and the albatross rots on the mirror.
Columbus struck his prow right through it,
en route to the New World's plunder,
but he liked the Sargasso—*blue as the sky
in Andalusia, fragrant as the air in Seville*—

the garbage sea, where the plastic of three continents
forms mats the breadth of Spain.

South of the plastic, offshore from Puerto Rico,
leptocephali ride on the Antilles current.
Feeding at night in the epipelagic, they in daylight
descend to the dark of Deep Scattering,
a phototaxic flight from the light and the deaths
that lurk there: harpooning cnidarians,
the grip-claws of krill, the lit jaws of the lanternfish—
devoured in centillions, centillions riding still.
A month or so since hatching, the size
of an April tadpole, they move in the plankton
like Pac-Man, simple machines of growth
and devouring, deliverers of the savage telos
written in their genes. They drift with the current,
making five or fifteen miles each day,
beyond Grand Bahama to the Blake Escarpment,
where the Florida current blows out from the strait
on the plume of Deepwater Horizon.
There, between Andros Island and Biscayne Bay,
it courses into the racing Antilles
to form the Gulf Stream, a roaring salt river
hurtling north on the edge of the American
continental shelf, its estuaries of blight:
oestrogen-saturated sewage, methamphetamine
neurotoxins, chromosome-warping
neonicotinoid run-off. The leptocephali soak it up,
and tumble to Hatteras with the flotsam
of the current—single-use Canaveral
space junk, the strip mall's car-tossed,
fast-food trash and radioactive manatees.

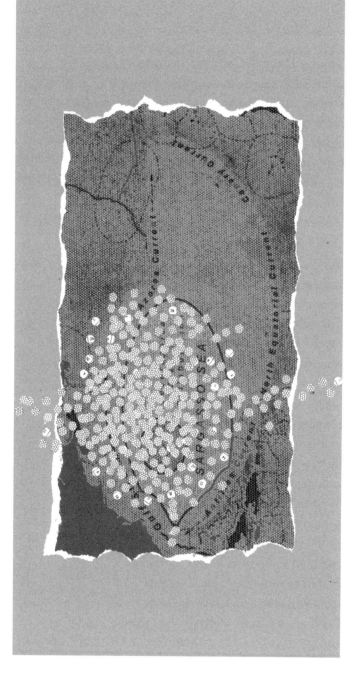

At Diamond Shoals, the Stream swerves north-east,
beyond Chesapeake Bay and the New York Bight
to the sea lanes over the Hudson Canyon.
There, in the diesel rumble of supertankers
and Liberian-registered Panamax freighters,
the leptocephali rise and fall, oblivious
to the onslaught: swarming capelin,
hoovering humpbacks, ravening hydrozoans—
CO_2 and CH_4, slicks of tank-flushed crude.
Every second of their journey is the first day
of the Somme, the annihilating batteries unrelenting.
But death is ocean's element, and blithe
the wide battalions ride, and redden their blades
in the ancient slaughter. Each life is built
from the bones of a billion dead,
and in their deaths are the murdered risen;
as long as the ocean circulates, eels
will find their way—but maybe, as the ice melts,
the current itself will stutter and dive,
and the larva slide to extinction's deeps
on the shelves of Atlantic's Niño.
For now they travel, and the broad shoals sail
off Nova Scotia and enter the Grand Banks'
desolate plateau, its right whale wrecks
and trawled-out, cod-less seas. Spectres wail
in the infrasonic, and ping their griefs
off the sonar's screen: for the live-plucked,
live-boiled auks of Funk, exterminated Beothuk
and the cleared and fly-tipped Gaels of Uist—
Whigs and Tories, their captains, crowns and thrones.

At Flemish Cap, the Trade Winds falter,
and the Labrador current pushes the Stream
out into the open ocean, where the salt river runs
in the zephyral flow of the thermohaline
North Atlantic Drift. Still bearing its load
of feeding leptocephali, the current fans out
through the lit pelagic in a delta of blooming phytoplankton
that stretches from Iceland to Western Sahara.
The central mass drifts east-north-east,
between the Azores and the Altair Seamount,
until west of Biscay and the Celtic Sea,
it passes over the grazing heights of the Porcupine Abyssal,
where, harried by cetorhines and schools
of swarming mackerel, the leptocephali
continue to travel and grow, rippling spearheads
of foliate gelatine, glittering in the half-lit heave
like a shoal of shredded cling-film.

By August, the wandering leptocephali
have arrived at the edge of the European shelf,
where they halt in the deeps off the Porcupine Seabight.
Now the length of an autumn stickleback,
they can grow no more and stop feeding.
For two-and-a half years, helpless drifters
on the gyre, they somehow drop invisible anchors
and hold against the flow. Here, in the twilit mesopelagic,
in the chemotaxic outflow of Shannon,
Severn and Seine, they hang in the heft
of the catalytic waters and begin the first metamorphosis.
Increased respiration metabolises fat
and excretes excess water; zigzag myomeres
harden to muscle and bone. Each polythene ribbon

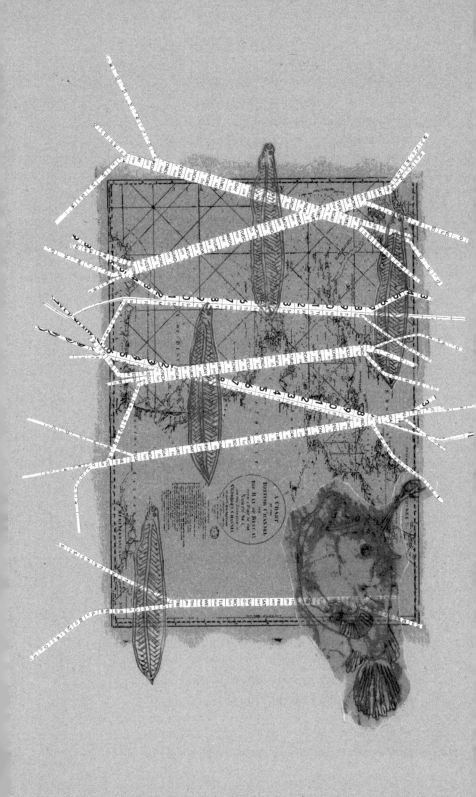

shrinks to a rubbery, see-through sea-snake,
thinner than an iPhone charging cable,
the length of my little finger—*glass eel*,
the microcosmic perfect form of the yellow eel
in its cave. An army of billions, stacked
offshore in the buffeting Drift and arrowed against the flow:
waiting for the occult sign that will herald
the surge into continental waters, each travelling
in the flexural power of its new undulatory wiggle.

Under the New Year's wintry constellations,
the glass eels begin their ascent.
Between the Porcupine Bank and the Goban Spur,
they emerge from submarine, deep-sea darkness
into the sunlit shallows of the Celtic Sea.
No longer the helpless, tropic flotsam
of the blown and thermohaline gyre,
they travel under their own steam, setting course
with the sextant of their mystic DNA.
Deep Scattering cannot hide them now,
from the predatory haddock and whiting,
sea bass, flounder and squid, so they travel by night
and bury themselves in the sea-bed's silts by day,
swimming against the tides and currents,
magnetised to their destinies in the scent
of distant rivers. The estuaries of the west—
Gironde and Tagus, Shannon, Severn and Seine—
swallow them in billions; but billions more
track east along the Channel, in the rumbling
diesel effluent of the 'busiest sea lane in the world',
its freight of towering container ships,
the rise and swell of Afghan refugees.

Onward they flow, making five or six miles daily:
over Hurd's Deep—where the MoD
dumped its phosgene shells and plutonium-239—
and the paleo-valleys and fossil meanders
of the Weichselian Glacial Maximum.
In the wreckage of Dunkirk and 1588,
they bury themselves among pieces of eight
and the little boat bones of drunken sailors.
The rivers of Wessex tempt some of them in,
but millions pass through Dover's straits
and into the German Sea. Once more they're changing,
darkening from head to tail, the glaze
becoming smoked and blurry—the glass eels
are transforming to *elvers*, gearing up for the move
into estuary and river, garbing themselves
in the colour of mud that for years will be their element.

Thames and Medway draw in their loads,
as do the southern fenland rivers,
but the vanguard of the shoal swims north,
some crossing to Rhine and Skaggerak,
the fjords of western Norway.
Millions more track the Danelaw's coasts,
in the lukewarm sump of the muck-brown seaside sea.
Too deep for Bempton's travelling gannets,
flatfish gulp them from the silts and gadoids
take their quotas. Past oil and gas rigs,
the trunks of turbines, in the estuarine scent
of *nearly there*, they straggle along the Lincolnshire coast
past Skeggy Butlins and Chapel St. Leonards,
to Ívarr's gap between Cleethorpes and Spurn:
where a column splits off and enters the Humber—
the end of their three-year saltwater journey.

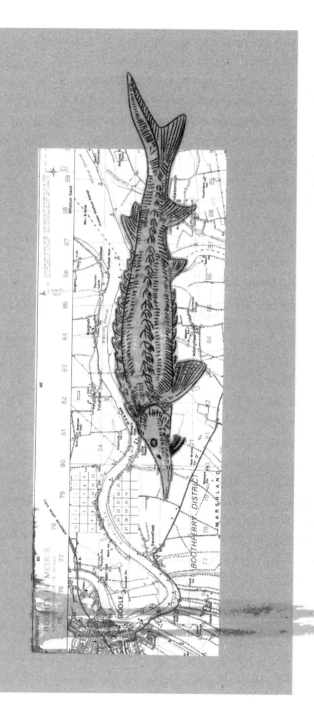

In the lanes where the pilots ply their trade,
the elvers divide on submarine shoals
to form cordons off Lindsey and York.
Armoured in mucus and toxic blood
against the hypotonic water and its pathogenic load,
they battle upstream in the brawling spate
of Three Ridings and Five Boroughs.
Harried by conger, crab and mullet,
herons and plunging grebes, the northern cordon
inches forward, under the mud-bank's steep phragmites,
past Skeffling Clays and Sunk Island Sands,
to the wharves and piers of the Port of Hull,
where they hide from the light in the dredgings of Empire:
bright litter of cod-skulls and cobbles of steam-coal,
uncoopered casks of rendered spermaceti.

Springtide sucks the elvers from the silts
and shoulders back the Humber. They ride
on the roar of the muscular bore to the sands
of Whitton Island, where the cordon splits once more.
A southern contingent is channelled mid-river
and into the Mercian Trent; the northern stream
flows along Faxfleet's shores and enters the Ouse
at the Blacktoft Channel. Great Ouse,
Eiríkr's dragon-prowed highway of commerce and blood,
where the Nassau-registered FRI Marlin
rides in the wake of the Humber Pride,
its cargo of half-pigs and Immingham diesel.
In the dark-moon growl of turning screws,
the elvers scale the wapentakes' flow
in a shock of suspended glyphosate
and the '62's condensed benzene.

At the reedbed's edge, black-headed gulls
come flocking and dipping; otters dive
in the turbid bounty and bitterns fill their crops.
Men with hand nets send the long shoal shattering.
A column along the Laxton shore straggles
upriver all summer, past the Port of Goole
and Howdendyke, to the confluence with Aire.
From there they'll travel north and west
into the PRIVATE salmon and brown trout streams
of Northfield's Tory sports day: Dales, Wolds and Moors.
But pressed against the western curve of Old Goole's
hooked meander, a depleted hundred-thousand ride
beneath the flood-wall's reedy strandline,
through sunken junk of fly-tipped prams
and bridge-tossed shopping trolleys.
There, between the Co-op and Vermuyden Terrace,
they pass into the Dutchman's canalised Don
and the drained and pumped, grid-linear waters
of the powerhouse West Riding, its bypasses
and business parks, sprawls of mortgaged housing.
Barely a cordon, hardly a shoal, they move into the kingdom
of the Amazon Fulfillment Centre, its clear-fell
devastation of investment, jobs and growth.

In the zero-hour run-off of link roads
and logistics, the elvers travel in dark solution,
past Decoy Farm and Rawcliffe Bridge,
under the M18. Below the floodbank
at Greenland Farm, anglers dip their poles.
Each elver's a little eel now, a *bootlace*,
the length and girth of an HB pencil,
knotting in its slime on the brandlinged hook

in the *yellow eel* livery of those seventies Ulleskelf years—
newt-brown uppers from nose-to-tail,
bacon-rind belly, flanks tinged with yellowy-green.
Recall the snake-head's underbite,
its saurian gaze and billowing gape
of breathing; those weird procellariid nostrils,
and the eye—bronze iris, black pupil,
a gaze from the depths of the Oligocene Tethys.
The hook's taken too deep and cannot be disgorged,
save with scissors or decapitating knife—
drops lopped into the river, vanishes in the flow.

The little eels swim past Went Green sluice
to the cormorant fields of Fishlake parish,
before crossing the cobbles of the submerged ford
into Bramwith by the oxbowed ings.
From here, most swim due south to Danum,
and beyond to the moorland heads of the river.
But in the shadow of the clap-cold cooling towers
of National Power's defunct Thorpe Marsh,
a trickle veers west through a hanging wooden floodgate,
exiting through the levee of the canalised Don
and passing between the levees of the canalised old Ea beck.

They don't know where they're going.
Not like the river-born, anadromous salmon,
homing upstream to their natal redds
along the madeleine scent of the current.
These eels were born in a continent of ocean
and their parents carried into that vastness
on mindless, reliable, pot-luck currents
from Iceland, Belgium, Tunisia, Spain.

Reliable gyres steer the rudderless broods
to their palaearctic landfall, where the elvers
ascend any freshwater outflow, from Hvita
on the Arctic Circle to Gueguerat
under the African Tropic of Cancer.
Ea's straggling cordon got here by chance,
their kin devoured by a hundred different *it'll do* rivers:
Al Khatt, Guadiana and Abhainn Mhor,
the big gapes of Tagus, Severn and Loire.

They don't know where they are.
The lit shallows run tepid but the bottoms
are cool and dark. The feeding is rich
and easy—roach fry, leeches, bivalves,
worms—so each little eel anchors
and runs its Miocene program: hide from light,
hunt at night, grow long and thick and fat.
The Ea is perfect, or would be, were it not
for the big eels—some three feet long
and thick as a man's wrist—long-rooted
in their benthic plots, snapping them up,
or sending them scooting upcurrent.

Thus the little eels travel, driven deeper
into the drainage, seeking a plot of their own.
Some strike it lucky, and courtesy of cormorant,
heron or otter, find vacant caves
under Marsh Lane bridge, just a hundred yards
from the floodgate. The rest trek on,
past Sickle Croft at Thorpe-in-Balne
and the power station settling ponds,
where huge pike haul down half-grown swans

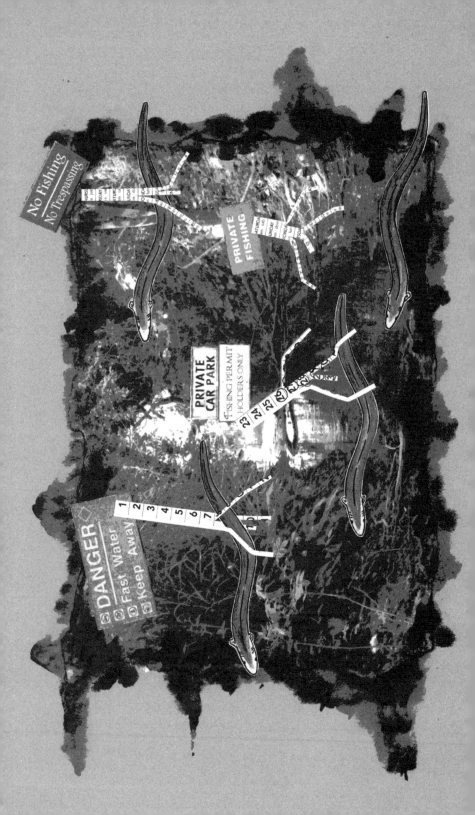

and full-grown crested grebes. There, in midnight
drenchings of summer thunder, some wriggle
through the grass of the sodden embankment
and squirm into the roots of the warm ponds'
deep phragmites. They'll trust blind chance
in the prowling murk and live on jack and fry.

From the Don to the A1(M), Ea flows
in its V between flat-topped mounds
dredged and piled by long-arm Komatsu crawlers.
The silts are dumped to dry out in the sun,
with their writhing collateral of suffocating eels.
In the filth and smashed flag, under squalls
of gulls and chancing crows, the survivors persist
in their straggling ascent, labouring the shallows
between moated Tilts and the ruin of Bentley Colliery,
its unpumped workings black with coal
and seams of dungeoned eels. What species
will they become there? What have they become
already—the legend of the Bentley Worm,
roaming the anthracite bowels of the earth
starved on the firedamp ghosts of miners,
emerging each Walpurgis Night from the depths
of the Welfare pit-pond, seizing tribute
from the ranks of the High Street's drunks
and the graveyard's coked-up, shrieking children.

Below Bullcroft tips at Carcroft common,
the beck runs under Watling Street
past the ASDA superstore and B&Q,
between Richard's Hampole and Robin Hood's Well.
In the approach to the thundering culvert

under the Doncaster-Wakefield road,
the Ea becomes the Hampole dike,
and in a fly-tipped paddock below the landfill,
finds, for the first time, its natural meander:
staggers of alder and tangled willow,
tussock-topped, flood-sheared cliffs.
The eels rest up in rat-holes, hunt fry
in the willows' cool shade: until something
in the water, or in the coding of their genes,
sends them questing against the current.
Another crawling culvert in the landfill's reek,
they exit to the light in a sheer-walled stream
between the London-Edinburgh railway line
and Stubbs Hall's leaky carp ponds:
blue shit seeped from chemical toilets,
cormorants dribbling lead. Rats feeding
from litter bins, discarded peg-side boilies.
The little eels slither in the crisp bag flow
and enter an ocean of drifting rape
where the dike water stinks like Roundup
and fitches—mink are patrolling the red-brick cave
under the shut-down colliery spur
of the shut-down Hull & Barnsley railway.
Darkness releases them into darkness,
the starless waters of Elmsall beck
in the stench of the Common End sewerage.
Now fifteen miles upstream from Don,
only a handful of eels remain of the hundreds
that passed the Thorpe-in-Balne control gate.
Nowhere to go now; in three or four miles
the map's fine blue line will fritter
in a maze of spring-fed trickles in the fields

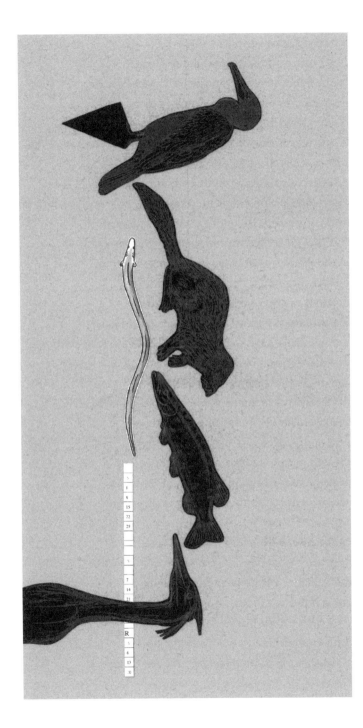

between Hemsworth and Kirkby.
But a quarter-mile beyond the sewerage,
in the flood-flattened rape below Lovatt's garage,
new water joins the flow—Frickley beck,
the barely-a-mile-long terminal flow
of a tangle of tiny dikes and streams that rise from the clays
between Watchcliff and Ringstone Hill.
A dozen or so divert and enter its current.
They wriggle along the flat-scraped silt
in the sheer–side drain of the embanked channel
and pass under the road to the ragwort horsefield
in the shadow of Frickley tips. Stridable stream,
meandering under the bankside hawthorns
in a foot or two of depth. Once a home
for watter rats and nesting bankside moorhens:
that was before the mink. But even in this desultory trickle,
with its workaday load of pesticides
and occasional blights of sewage,
the waterworld's intact: you can still tickle trout,
and river fish flee before your bootsteps—
dace and gudgeon, bullhead and barbel,
the odd patrolling pike. And eels, of course,
buried under banks, in the clefts of rootballs,
wherever the beck finds a yard or so of depth.

At the tunnel-lip under the H&B spur,
only three from Sargasso remain to complete
their ascent. The downstream dredging
killed hundreds of eels and some of the new ones
took their vacant places. Herons prowl
this easy water, and mink work the pool
at the step of the tunnel, where the travelling eels

are forced to attempt a grass snake's slithering ascent.
Only one makes it through and into Frickley Park.
Here the beck widens and deepens for a stretch,
as the flow backs up from the arch of the tunnel.
The stream cuts across the pylon field
between banks of nettles and the bollarded stumps
of hawthorns. The surviving eel swims forward,
winding between the banks, seeking a plot
in which she can anchor for the next fifteen or twenty years.
She sniffs the waters with her periscope nostrils,
wriggles into root knots and under debris-dams.
This stream has good feeding, bloodworm,
caddis and fry; but already there are eels here,
with gapes wide enough to swallow her skinny
nine inches whole; they loom from darkness,
lunging and biting, taking chunks from her caudal
and ventral fins, chasing her on upstream.

Where the beck is straightened along Frickley Lane
she crawls along the ballasted shallows
under a wall of gabioned limestone.
Here the waters flow fast and broken,
as the tumbling spate of Holywell beck
roars into the flow from a concrete pipe
and roils in its rumbling plunge pool.
The stones of the bridge the pipe replaced,
along with the swallow's nest, crusted to the ashlar,
were abandoned in the flow to cause this foaming turbulence.
The eel flashes under the feral white water
and slides into the flat-bottomed, deep-cut race
that glints through the lattice of slashed-back quick
a fathom below the lane. Hard-banks here,

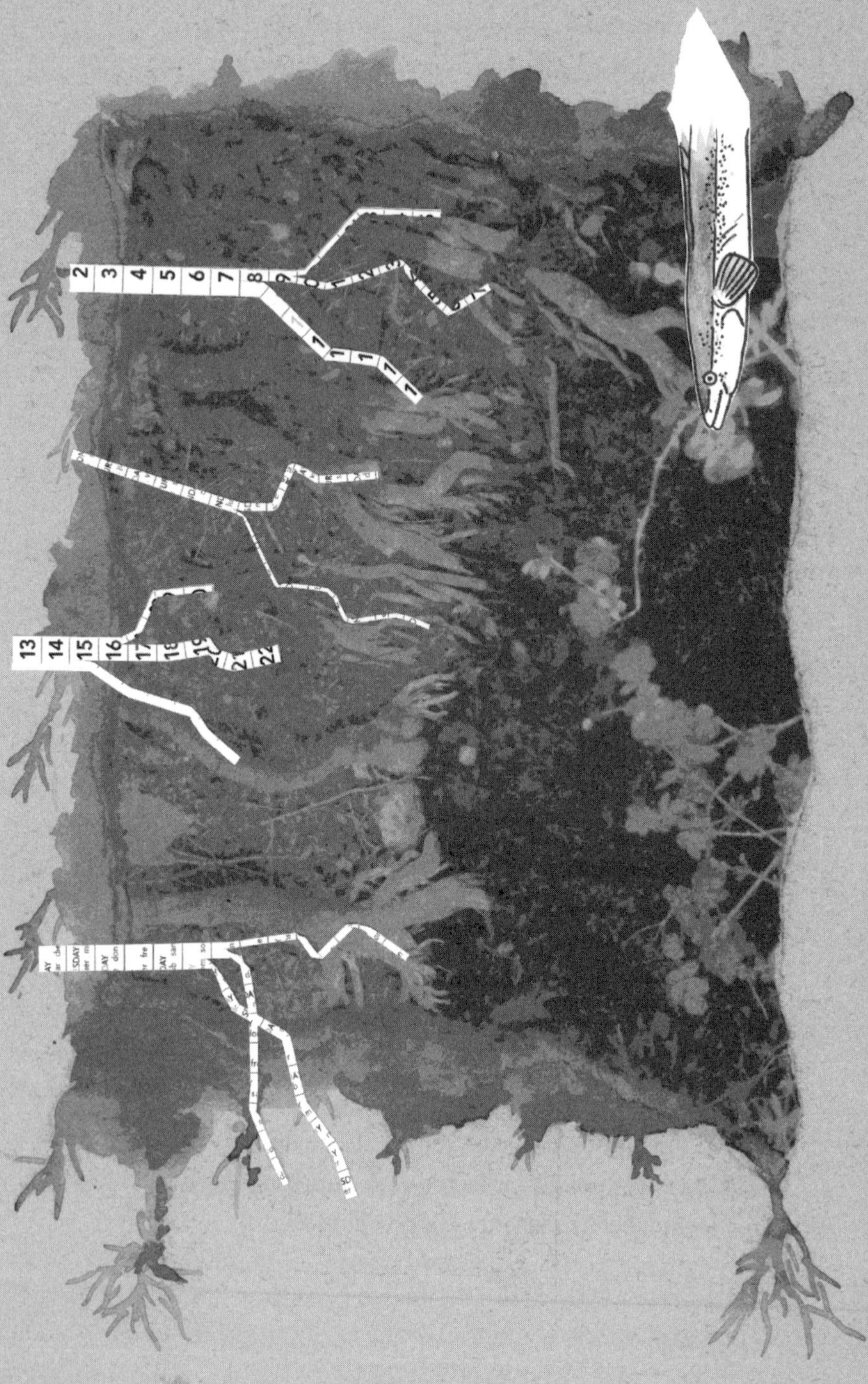

no shelter, but shortly the stream begins to widen
and find a little depth: another pipe,
another plunge pool, at the gateless gap
facing Hooton Thorn Covert, on the point
of the nameless fox-head wood. Waist-deep
and wide enough for a man to float on his back
like Jesus. The covert side grassy, unhedged;
the lane side a hedge of splintered hawthorn
and the overhang gloom of a sycamore.
She reaches the pipe-lip, only inches above
her surface-breaking head, submerges
and circles the pool. Beneath the pipe-drop's
trickle of fall, a dark eel rises, lunging
from the rubble towards her. She flicks off
in a plume of silt, and continues her circling
in the sycamore's shadow, snaking the caves
of the submarine rootball—rat smells,
trout smells, effluent from the Landrace piggery,
stinks of dead pigeon, pheasant and crow.
Bloodworm, caddis and fry. Eel smell—
but no incumbent eel. So under the bank
of Frickley beck, by the gateless gap
at Hooton Thorn Covert, on the point
of the nameless fox-head wood, she reaches the end
of her forty-month journey. She knots her tail
in a crevice of the rootball and pokes out
her gape in a predatory billow of breathing.
Now she waits, and rests.

Sunday morning, twelfth of May, 2019: I pulled from
the pool the eBay crab pot and saw her knotting in the
sock. The first one I'd caught since the Ulleskelf bootlace
of 1977—which I disgorged by lock-knife decapitation,
the custom at the time. I unzipped her into the waiting
bucket and walked a beaming mile along the lane to the
verge where I'd parked the car—they're still here!

The tank had been ready for a month, but the eels—
in Went and Ea and Howell becks—weren't taking my
Tesco fish-counter bait, and I started to wonder if their
inexhaustible biomass had become exhausted already. But
maybe the water was just too cold, or the whiffy sprats
just too long dead. 48 x 18 x 15 inches, 200 hose-piped
litres, bedded on one-inch polystyrene on top of the garage
shoe cupboard. Three inches of gravel, a cave of broken
potsherds. Oxygenating Ranunculus, Elodea canadensis.

I tipped her in, and watched her circle in whiplash
panic the walls of her glassy cage. 'Just for the summer,'
I told her. 'Just for the poem. You'll be back in your pool
by autumn.' And I flattened my palm against the glass
in a gesture of reassurance. But that only made it worse,
so I stepped back from the tank to remove my threat and
watched from a perch on the dog crate. After a while she
seemed to settle and peered out from her potsherd cave.
'Ella,' I said, and was mightily pleased with myself—
until I remembered Mijbil and Toki and Christian the
Hugging Lion. So I stuck with the name I'd started to
call her already—little eel.

After three days my little eel had made herself at home, poking her head out from under the potsherds and kneading her gills in a pleated billow of breathing. She didn't seem to mind me, unless I rearranged the furniture of the tank or lurched before the glass. I put in a red bulb, pulled up a stool, and watched. Mostly she'd just burrow in the substrate—a plunging whip-crack pluming silt, rattling the glass with gravel, then poke out her head from the stones: blank Miocene gaze, gaped underslung hook-jaw and that metronome billow of breathing. Sometimes in the dark-room darkness she'd loop her infinities over the gravels and snake to the top of the water. Once she stretched full-length along the pane and allowed me to tape her measurements: nineteen inches, thick as a garden hosepipe—so conceivably a he, even from the catchment's far extremity. But something seemed off about her yellow eel livery. The upperparts were a little too dark, and a bloom of bronze seemed to shine from her gills and neck. Not like I remembered from the Wharfe or the Went, or like the exemplars on Google Images. I put it down to natural variation, and brought her food.

I fed her every day. She was a picky eater, rejecting sprats and mackerel chunks, strips of beef and blocks of frozen shrimp—too dead, too foreign to her beck-raised habit. The live food I provided—bloodworm, mussels, tadpoles and fry, including an inch-long perfect pike— disappeared from the tank, but I never saw her make a kill, or caught her eating anything else but earthworms. She'd only take the big ones, the six-inch crawlers. I'd lower them slowly over her head. They'd be wriggling before her and suddenly   vanished—an

*echo of gulp, faint ripple in the water—Miocene gaze,
gaped underslung hook-jaw, that metronome billow of
breathing. She'd take three or four in quick succession,
then nothing for two or three days or more, despite my
efforts to tempt her. Tank bottom strewn with waving
chironomids, limp streamers of bleached lumbricus.*

*Mid-June, her eating had become erratic and the gaps
between feeding grew longer. Come July, she was fasting
for two or three weeks at a time. A whisper between my
temples—you're making her ill—take her back to her
pool or you'll kill her. I gazed for confirmation. She
gazed right back—Miocene gaze, underslung hook-jaw,
that metronome billow of breathing. No telepathy,
no communion. She lived her life in the jaws of a
cormorant, and I was nothing but a heretic cormorant,
one that toyed and would not kill, unaccountably parallel
with her living. Miocene gaze, underslung hook-jaw,
metronome billow of breathing.*

*By August she'd changed her skulking habit, and spent
her days hanging tall in the height of the tank, anchored
in the gravel by the tail. And her yellow eel livery was
definitely off—her back was dark, her belly pale, and her
gills were glinting like foil—was she silvering? I couldn't
be sure: I'd not seen a silver eel for over 40 years, since
Julius foul-hooked that storied two-pounder at Smeaton
on the Went; so I dropped my eBay pot once more, to
compare and contrast.*

*In the tank together, the difference was clear. The new
eel was riverine yellowy-green. Little eel was transforming
into her guillemot ocean livery. Maybe that's why her
eating had become erratic—perhaps she'd begun to absorb
her gut as she started her metamorphosis—though she*

took out a chunk from the interloper before I took it back.

In August, she ate nothing at all. 'Let her go,' the whisper said. 'It's cruel to keep her confined in that tank in the gloom of the garage. She's pining for the length of the river, that's why she won't eat.' Anchored in the gravel, billowing her breathing, fixed in that Miocene stare. Getting darker, paler and mackerel metallic and even her eyes were boggling larger. There was no doubt about it. In a month she'd be ready to set out for Sargasso.

So I netted her from the tank and tipped her in the bucket and walked the lane to the pool on the point of the fox-head wood: where I crouched in the shade of the bankside sycamore and prepared to empty her in; and where I hesitated, and touched her for the first time, sending her circling the bucket in panic; and so had to reassure her, explaining that I meant no harm, then and in the period of her kidnap and captivity. And I explained to her why I'd done what I'd done, and that I hoped she understood, and that she might remember me, because I would certainly remember her; and that maybe, someday, it might fall to either one of our fates to be called to help the other, in this world, or the subtle world of spirit. And so I said goodbye to my little eel, and emptied her into the culvert's plunge-pool, where she unwound down in the darkling waters and vanished in the caves of the sycamore's submarine rootball.

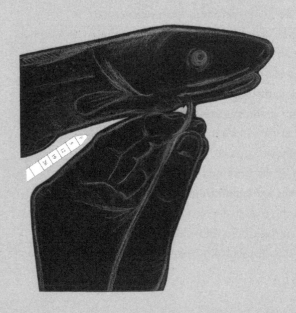

Late September dark moon. Thunderheads
massing and snarling. She stirs in her cave
in the sycamore rootball. Her black and silver skin is tight,
her rippling snake-flesh slick with gleaming fat.
She lifts her head and breathes the water,
kneading her long pectorals. Eyes like oversized
pilot goggles, clapped to the sides of her head,
rods supplanting cones in the second transformation.
She perceives only light and darkness now,
the spatial acuity of predatory vision
a redundant inefficiency: six thousand
black and fasting miles to the spawning grounds
of the southern Sargasso, over the edge of the Nares Abyssal,
south-east of the Bermuda Ridge.
She stretches her length from the submarine tangle
and tastes the turbulent, swollen waters—
recoils from dusk-light dimming overhead.
Winds restless through the maze of roots and snags.

Stacked cumulonimbus, blacked-out
constellations. Hammering rain, stripping
the leaves from the sycamores. Field drains foaming
with tilth in suspension. Beck risen to the arch
of the culvert pipe, leaf-litter corkscrewing
under the tunnel in a roaring Coriolis whirlpool.
She stretches again from her submarine rootball
to sniff in the whelming flow: Nitram, Roundup,
Viroxide Super, Supalyx equine mineral-lick—
the olfactory blur of migrating silver eels.
She unknots her tail and abandons her length
to the current—flung rope in the torrent,
hurtling with the debris in suspension—black blizzards
of leaves and broken-off branches, cannoning
bottles and tins. Flushed through culverts
and under bridges, bent forests of bulrush and torn-off
mats of flag, she's thundered across the inundated common
to the maelstrom confluence with Elmsall beck,
where a stubblefield lake is expanding upstream
in the whiff of the sewerage outflow;
eel stink tumbling blindly beside her,
grey froth of used condoms and sanitary towels.
Ghostly vortex of mewling black-head gulls.

Shot out from the H&B culvert like a cork,
she rides the torrent to Carcroft Common
where the Ea has broadened to thirty feet
and is overtopping its light industrial floodbanks.
Sodium streetlights glower in siling darkness,
but the pummelling current of black whitewater
is too strong to be resisted. She's swept on the surge
to the confluence with Don, sheer volume of flood

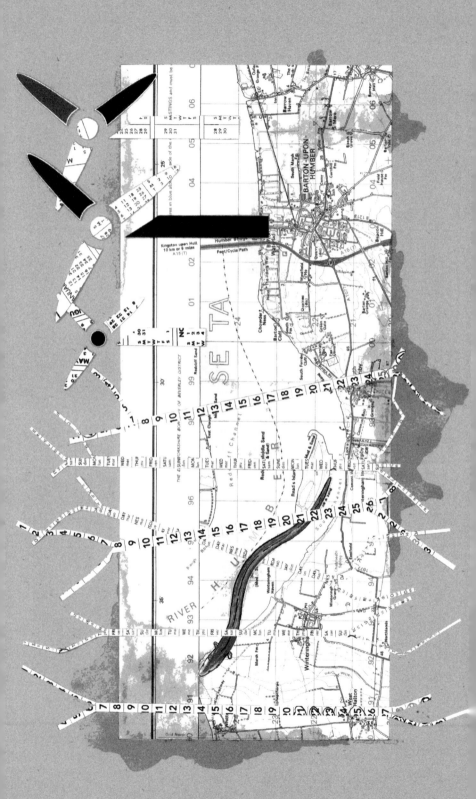

backing up at the pipe, a surface-breaking,
wrestling shoal of stymied silver eels—
but the gate's slammed open by the force of the flux
and the suck of the distant German Sea.
She javelins through and enters the river,
having ridden the spate for sixteen miles
in less than half a night. No weirs on her rivers,
nor Archimedes Screw, men with fyke or wing nets.
Darkness and spate keep the herons from hunting;
pike beat their gills in the shelter of tributary streams.
The only hazards are collision and stranding.

Don racing with pallets and sundered
bankside trees. Unmoored narrowboat,
akimbo on the current. River lit
with invisible glitter; thousands of silver eels,
careering under Rawcliffe Bridge,
past the brimming drains of Decoy Farm,
to the swollen Ouse at the Port of Goole.
Broad river bellowed to the flat of its levees,
freighted with lumber and propane bottles,
loosed jetties and half-sunk cruisers.
Mute swans huge on the dark meniscus,
excited greylag, trumpeting overhead.
Eels from Derwent, Aire and Nidd,
the trickles of Peak, Dales, Wolds and Moors,
are carried downstream to the Danelaw's
vast collision of current: Trent Falls,
where tonnage of tumbling Mercian eels
join to form the swollen Humber's catadromous flow.
Spate shoves the ebbing tide downstream
from Whitton to Saltend Chemical Park,

where dawn breaks and the sea shoves back.
She sinks with the shoal in the silts of the P&O sea-lane,
and buries herself in the suction-dredged deep sands.

In estuarine gloom, tight in her tunnel
in the submarine muck, she braces herself
against the flood and calibrates her taxes.
Atlantic salt in procellariiform nostrils
and her glass eel's imprinted geomagnetic memory
lay down her path before her. She pokes out her head
and waits for the tide to turn: Miocene gaze,
underslung hook-jaw, metronome billow of breathing.
The sonic assaults of the thundering Humber—
huge screws of the MV Olympic Legacy,
the diesel reverb of the Pride of Zeebrugge—
send shock waves down her lateral line
and rattle the bones of her fine-tuned inner ear.
The back-flushed sewage of the Pride of Hull
settles its stink in the wormy silts around her.
Harbour seals rummage in the sunken filth,
plucking out shellfish, flounder and eel.
Shoals of predatory mullet and bass,
cormorants and divers attendant: the benthic ghost
of a twenty-five-foot sturgeon. Draws in her head,
hides in the dark till darkness.

Sucked out of her socket in the ebb-tide's gloom,
she sets her compass south past Spurn
and for six hours swims with the drag
of the seaward current. In the fifteen-fathom
bombing range offshore from Donna Nook,
the ebb-tide stalls and the flow turns back to Humber.

She sits out the flood in her sea-floor sangar,
Thunderbolt autocannon ripping overhead,
torpedo shoals of arrowhead coley,
exploding in the silts—from Silver Pit
to Southern Bight, the sea-bed's combed
with the bivouacs of eels, each one aimed blind
in its Tomahawk head for the hypertonic waters
of Sargasso. They labour tidal miles twice-daily,
a shallow-sea trudge to the race of the open Atlantic.
Some stumble in the water column
like warfarin-poisoned rats, swim bladders blown
by the *Anguillicola* nematode,
unable to make either current or anchor—
gulped down by shoals of cruising cod,
the baleen gapes of minkes. Skate and dogfish
take their tolls, the maws of white-beaked dolphins,
but only a week after leaving her cave
she's travelled the length of the Saxon Shore
to the undersea forest of turbine towers
at Vattenfall's Thanet Wind Farm.
Squeezed into a crack in the concrete foundation,
she breathes in capital's benzoylecgonine outflow,
the insufflated pisspots of Parliament and City:
hyperactivity, degeneration, cardiac distress.
Resisting infection and chemical assault,
she passes through the White Cliffs' garrisoned straits
into hyperactive sea-lanes—renownèd, stubborn as Jewry.

I'm making it up as they go along.
Almost nothing demonstrated, almost
everything inferred. Once in the ocean,
they disappear completely, the odd accidental

in a fisherman's net, off Brittany, Brindisi;
tagged experimental fish, lost in the Waddenzee;
undigested predated fish, cut from the guts
of Azorean cachalots and googly-eyed cod
longlined off Kilda. The leptocephalus data-sets
Schmidt produced from Dana's trawls
led to a certain hypothesis: eels spawn
in the depths of the southern Sargasso
and their highway to and from there
is the North Atlantic Gyre—where not a single
anguillid eel has ever been caught or seen.
'Somehow', then, along the Channel,
dragged limp on dark and ebbing tides—
or hard-gained miles in the pummelling face of flood.
Avoiding the light and its armies of killers
past Brighton and the Isle of Wight,
she snakes in the murk of the bottoms by day
and rises into the tidal race at night—
each phototaxic diurnal dive getting deeper
by the day, as English coasts decline
to vast Atlantic. Past Portland and Cotentin,
she swims above the seabed silts
in seventy or eighty fathoms of murk,
through the wreckage of Affray and Sala's Piper Malibu,
down the slope of the Biscay shelf
to the bottomless tohuwabohu of ocean.
Faint eel scent wafts along the Channel
from the west; migrants from Baltic,
Rhineland and Gaul, ahead of her
on their journey. But there is no shoal,
no synchronous tonnage of travelling fish,
to be picked up on sonar and hoovered

into holds, like the sand-lance of Dogger,
or Madeiran sardines—she's making her own way,
one of ten, or five hundred million, vanished
in the vastness of *oceanus incognitus*,
blind to the lung-tethered lubbers on land,
the white-coats and accountants of the inventoried seas.

Sometimes on her journey, eel scent surges,
and she senses along her lateral line
the congenial electricity of a fellow nuptial pilgrim.
For minutes, hours or even days, until one lags,
or a marlin's intervention, she'll wind in time
with her dark companion, twin sextants set
for the distant warm salt sea. If she had eyes
designed to see, and not those supersized,
glaucous goggles, fit only to meter the lux
of the undersea light, she'd see her counter-shaded,
epipelagic self—black-backed, white-bellied,
long-finned like a winter puffin—a glint
in the squint of submarine darkness, occulted
in that world—but not to the scabbardfish
or bluefin tuna, grey seal or bottlenose dolphin,
zooming from the gloom along the widening Channel,
to the cliff of the Shamrock Canyon.
Here, in the three-mile plummet to the Biscay Abyssal,
seal and dolphin return to their harbours
and scabbardfish sink to their depths;
but the bluefin persist into open ocean,
harrowing the holocaust photocline with xiphius,
macrocephalus, savage architeuthis.

Heading south-west on her entorhinal compass,
she senses the Grand Banks' salts in suspension
and enters the deep, olfactory race
of the thermohaline Azores current—
the north-eastern curve of the North Atlantic Gyre,
her fast track to Sargasso. Fifteen, twenty,
maybe twenty-five miles a day,
over the Azorean Fracture Zone
and the rise of the Meteor Seamount.
Loose in the flow, swimming or steering,
under shoals of scad and bubble-net humpbacks,
she joins the southbound Canary current
between Desertas and La Palma,
over the northern Cape Verde Plain.
Loose in the flow, swimming or steering,
twenty-five, thirty, maybe fifty miles a day,
across dark continents of plummeting water
where serpents vent from the smoking depths
of a sea-floor white with shackled blacks
and the wrecks of harpooned whales.
High over the collateral wastes of Empire,
a cordon is forming in the breadth of the current—
six hundred miles wide, a quarter-mile deep
and fifteen hundred miles in length.
Unnumbered millions of travelling eels,
flickering in the heave like flecks of lint,
dim ripples of the soaring constellations
their eyes have never seen. Transatlantic 747s
curve blind skies above them; Seawolves prowl
the opaque depths below: they have ceased to exist
in our world. But in theirs she's getting closer
to her amniotic graveyard heiron—she can smell it

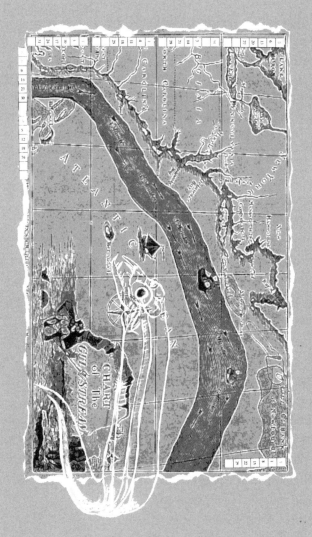

in the waters, sense it in the stars,
feel it in the needle of her geomagnetic cortex—
electrochemical calibrations, sparking in the dark.

Offshore from San Antão, the buffeting Trade Winds
shoulder the flow in a swerve across the ocean:
the North Equatorial Current, Atlantic's conveyor
to the dark Antilles, two-and-a-half thousand
blind sea miles at thirty or fifty a day.
The cordon narrows in the curve of the current,
and there, between the fifteen/twenty latitude lines
at two hundred and fifty fathoms of depth,
she senses for the first time, her fellow-travelling,
deep-spaced shoal: an ultrasound cacophony
of directional undulations, nerves tingling in the skin;
mucus chemtrails, heavy with hormones,
flooding the cells with sex; the muscular push
and billow of breathing, sometimes swimming
beyond or beside her, intersecting electrical vectors,
charging her aura, driving her on.

She's heavy with three or four million eggs
now, her white-kid belly deep-keeled
from throat to vent. Posterity's vessel,
she's reducing herself to the seed of her species' future,
every non-essential body-part—eyes and bones,
digestive tract—recycling to gonads and roe.
She's close to exhaustion, her energies almost spent.
Eight months and six thousand fasting miles
on the self-immolatory, pelican fuel
of the flesh of her gourmet body.
She ropes on through the water that buoys her,

the current she rides upon, over the rise
of the Atlantic Ridge, where thermal vents
and magma plumes infuse the shivering water column
with the signature iron and magnesium taste
of the molten basalt mantle—her imprinted
larval hippocampus knows she's almost there.
In the drench of natal metals in suspension
she crosses into the Antillean Atlantic
in the last of her swimming strength,
encountering the heat and salinity fronts
that tell her, at last, she's arrived at the place
of her birth and programmed death:
the Subtropical Convergence Zone
of the southern Sargasso, 17 degrees north,
59 degrees west, two hundred and fifty miles
east of Anguilla, where the inside curve
of the gyring current tears at the edge
of the brooding Miocene waters.
She parks in the current at fifteen hundred feet
and begins her transformation.

Waning gibbous, 71% visible, stacked banks
of cumulonimbus. Black ocean humping
and breaking. Taiwanese canning ships,
upping their nets, heading for Leeward harbours.
Skeins of pelicans straggling over dissipating wakes.
Darkness in all directions: firefly twin-props
winking overhead, soft neon of turquoise myctophids,
dimming from the deeps—barracudina,
onychoteuthis, a blizzard of marine snow—
and under the photocline's abyssal blackness,
livid as knife scars, or threadworms

in the water, a vast raft of drifting eels,
scattered across the Convergence Zone
like buffalo, or passenger pigeon,
two or three every fifty or a hundred yards
for two hundred thousand cubic miles of ocean.
She travels on the Antillean flow at twenty
or thirty miles a day, drenched in the scent
of her gleaming congeners, in the rush
of her oestrogen-saturated blood.
Cachalots cruise and tarpon loom,
but all her attention is inward now,
as her DNA completes the reprogramming
of her body, transforming it into a breeding machine.
The remnant nanograms of skeletal calcium
and the adipose fats from the wastes of her muscles
dissolve in the blood and transport
to the oocytes, which swell red gold
and ripen, flushing the pleated kid of her belly,
pressing against her oviduct's tingling trapdoor.
Blood bulges the loosening lips of her cloaca
and bruises the ventral fin red/blue.
She hangs in her depths like a Universe,
and waits to come into her Queendom.

A half-mile distant, an eighteen-inch male
is plundering his carcase to complete his transformation.
The remaining lipids of his glands and organs,
his muscular proteins and the minerals of his bones,
are transported to the gonads and repurposed
to spermatogenesis, shoaling his belly with milt.
His silver eel livery blackens to carbon steel;
a finger-thin stripe from throat to vent

is all that remains of his wintry guillemot belly.
Blood-red speckling, vasodilated vent,
scarlet ventral and caudal fins. Hooked kype
like an upstream salmon. Blood banging
in the brain. He rides the towering
mesopelagic, searching in the darkness.

She's travelling west-by-north with the current,
a curve offshore from Windward.
Swollen like a pomegranate, her roseate coelom
thick with eggs, each microscopic seed
of blood lit in its aril of vitelline gold.
She winds in the flow like a length of fraying halyard,
the edge of coming apart. He's swimming
a hundred yards behind her, locked on
to her oestrogen contrail. They drift for days
on the whelming current, moving deeper
into the fabled sea: 19 degrees north, 61 west,
approaching the rise of the Puerto Rico Trench,
a hundred miles north of Barbuda.
Blue-blackness above; black-blackness below:
waning crescent, 24% visible, faint glow
of Deep Scattering's bioluminescence.
Diesel growl of longliners, trolling snoods
for snapper. Humpback and pilot whales,
wahoo and marlin, picking off the bounty—
a continent of eels coming into fruition
as far as fancy's lightless eye can see:
little males, fourteen-inch veterans
of the hemispheric journey, hanging limp
in the drift like branches of flaccid sargassum,
completing their nuptial transformations;

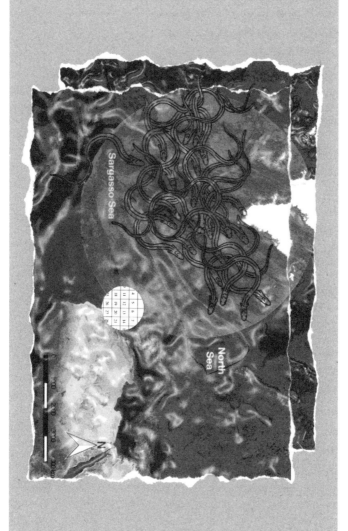

others, already come into their ripeness,
are riding the pheromone bow-waves of females,
girthy as pythons, four or five feet long.
Soft explosions of pluming milt
flare from mesopelagic darkness,
as all around them, eels entwine
and jettison their loads. The water stinks of sex
and death—progesterone, testosterone,
ichthyotoxic blood. She shivers in the warm,
aphrodisiac current, every nerve-end tingling,
each tender tip engorged. He's drifting in her orbit now,
homed in on her cloacal trail. He loops
his snaky electron around her—she recoils,
and snaps her gaping, rat-trap jaw—not ready.
So for the moment they simply swim together,
the nineteen-inch female, her underslung bicep of belly,
and her swollen bootlace suitor. They drift
with the current deep into black Sargasso.

20 degrees north, 62 west.
The outer rise of the Puerto Rico Trench,
a hundred miles north of Anguilla.
New Moon, 1% visible. Kraken darkness,
lit only by octopus phosphorescence
and the bright detonations of ejaculating eels.
They've been travelling in tandem for five days now,
through frittering flames of fertilised ova
and the disarticulate, space-junk fall
of dead and dying eels. This is their predestined,
inescapable fate, the fate of every Atlantic eel
since the Yucatan asteroid dropped its apocalypse
fifty million years ago—to ruin themselves

in the act of breeding and die in the dopamine afterglow,
drifting down from the towering heights of ocean
to the black red clays of the five-mile abyss,
layer upon layer upon googolplexian layer.
Their bodies are coming apart, held together
only by shrink-wrapped skin and the kamikaze
cerebellum that tells them *live!*—to breed and die.
They're running on neurosteroids now,
their muscular strength exhausted— it's now or never.
But her biochemical transformation
is finally complete—the dark-moon shudders
in her teleost womb and she's suddenly wreathed in sex.
He stiffens and begins his dance around her,
nosing the waters, advancing and retreating
in a tentative submarine hokey-cokey;
like he's scared to get close, like he's got
at least one glaucous eye on that gaping, rat-trap jaw.
She drifts and ignores him, gaping and closing
that rat-trap jaw, beckoning him forward,
until he finally plucks up the courage to touch,
coming under and rubbing her pulsing belly
with the nacelles of his head. He kneads the flesh
of her underbody with a zig-zag massage
from pleated throat to vent. She gapes and twitches, swims,
and for a while they swim touch-tight together,
him coiling his cable around the rope
of her body, constricting and releasing,
bringing her to the edge. She gapes and twitches,
apparently impassive—but a landslide has started
inside her. He uncurls his coils and once more
swims beneath her, nuzzling at her leaking vent
like a Typhoon fuelling from a stratotanker,

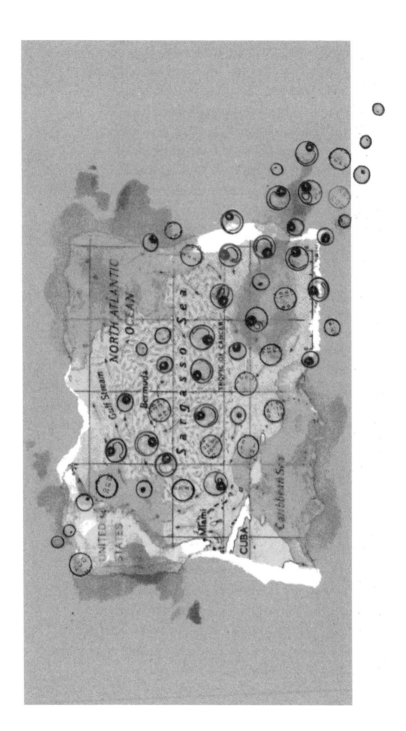

butting the bulge of her loosening roe sac,
triggering the sensory overload that will release
them both into the ecstasy of body, the DMT
and oxytocin rush of coitus and extinction.
Milt pumps down the tube of his urethra
and backs up at the sphincter of the vent;
he stiffens and ejaculates a depth charge
blast of sperm. She shivers and her gold load slides.
They couple in the milt cloud, lit in the shock
of its bloom—once more he's frotting the flange
of her vent and butting the walls of her coelom,
once more he ejaculates—again, and again—
until the hypertonic waters are smoking
with milt, and her shuddering body
can hold it back no longer. She cracks like a whip
and her body convulses, spurting gusher
after gusher of glittering golden ova,
sparks from the cornucopian flame
of Archaea's unkillable, dark pleroma,
quickening through the mist of sperm and rising
through the photocline to join the thermonuclear
microplankton of the drifting epipelagic.

Glossary and Notes

PAGE NINE. 'The European eel' (*Anguilla anguilla*) is a critically endangered fish that until the 1980s made up to 50% of the piscine biomass in some river systems. In England, eels were staples of the national diet and economy until well into the 20ᵗʰ century, and were so common (and valuable) that many estates and individuals paid their rents and taxes in eels. Over the last fifty years, European eels have experienced a catastrophic decline, with recruitment of young eels to some catchments reduced by 99%. The species was added to the Convention of International Trade in Endangered Species (CITES) Appendix II in 2007, and to Annex B of the EU's Wildlife Trade Regulations in 2009, both listings having the effect of banning international trade in the species. In 2013 the European eel was assessed as 'Critically Endangered' by the International Union for Conservation of Nature and Natural Resources (IUCN) and placed on its 'Red List'. The reasons for the European eel's decline are still not fully understood, but include a range of anthropogenic factors, including pollution; the impact of the absorption of chemicals, drug metabolites and heavy metals on the fish's physiology and reproductive capacity; commercial over-exploitation; drainage of marsh and fen; intensive management of waterways; fragmentation of river catchments by weirs, dams and hydro-electric plants; debilitation by introduced parasites; and the impact of global warming on ocean currents and spawning conditions.

The **Subtropical Convergence Zone** (STCZ) of the **southern Sargasso**—a vast area, comprising hundreds of thousands of cubic miles of ocean—is the spawning ground of the European eel. The STCZ has three main characteristics that make it attractive to eels: the water is warm, allowing rapid embryonic and larval development; ocean currents bring nutrients which enable the proliferation of the zooplankters on which the larval eels feed; and the currents transport the larval and juvenile eels to the European estuaries and rivers in which they will spend the majority of their adult lives.

Until the 20th century, the life cycle of the European eel was a mystery. In natural conditions, anguillid eels only become sexually mature in the depths of the ocean (to this day, no-one has ever encountered a sexually mature European eel outside of a laboratory aquarium). This led to the development of a range of theories about the origins of eels, from Aristotle's contention that they emerged from 'the bowels of the earth' to speculations that they developed from horsehair, or freshwater worms, or that they gave birth to live young at multiple, unknown, offshore locations.

In 1922, the work of the great Danish biologist, Johannes Schmidt (building on the previous work of Francesco Redi, Carlo Mondini, Johann Kaup, Giovanni Grassi, Salvatore Calandruccio and others) culminated in his identification of the Sargasso as the spawning ground of the European eel. Schmidt did not physically discover spawning eels in the Sargasso. He came to his conclusion by systematically measuring eel larvae in the Northern Atlantic and concluded that the area where he found the smallest (the most recently hatched) was the most likely spawning ground. Subsequent research has refined and confirmed Schmidt's findings and although spawning has still not been observed, it is virtually certain that the European eel breeds in the STCZ, north of the Windward Islands, 50–70 degrees west and 20–30 degrees north.

The Sargasso Sea is a discrete body of twenty-five million years old water located roughly in the middle of the North Atlantic Ocean. It is the only sea that is entirely bordered by water—the current system of the North Atlantic Gyre, which circles around it, fraying its edges, but effectively corralling its warm, highly saline waters, and preventing them from mixing with the generalised Atlantic water mass. Roughly the size of the United States, the Sargasso lies off the continental shelves of North America, Greenland and northern Europe, west of the northern mid-Atlantic Ridge.

Marine **snow** is a continuous shower of organic detritus falling from the upper layers of the water column; eels probably spawn at around **fifteen hundred feet**. The ocean is divided into five broad layers, related to depth and the degree to which sunlight can penetrate. The photic layer, from the surface to around 200m, is known as the **epipelagic**. Below the epipelagic is the *mesopelagic*, which extends to 1000 metres. Although some light penetrates the upper reaches of the mesopelagic, it is essentially dark. Leptocephali travel in the upper mesopelagic and the lower epipelagic. Adult European eels migrate in the mesopelagic and probably spawn in its upper reaches. The other ocean layers are the *bathypelagic*, the *abyssopelagic* and the *hadalpelagic*.

TEN. **Eighteen-degree water** is a body of water in the Sargasso that maintains the constant temperature implied by the name even when surrounding waters are much colder. The life-cycle of the European eel has eight, or possibly nine phases: 1. birth in the Sargasso and existence as a **leptocephalus**; 2. migration into continental waters as a leptocephalus; 3. metamorphosis of the leptocephali into minute transparent eels (glass eels), which soon gain pigment, and are then referred to as elvers; 4. invasion or ascent by elvers into estuaries and freshwater systems; 5. metamorphosis of the elvers into yellow eels; 6. growth of yellow eels in estuaries and freshwater systems; 7. metamorphosis of yellow eels into silver eels, and the development of male or female sexual maturity; 8. reproductory migration (or descent) of silver eels from freshwater to the Sargasso, during which a further metamorphosis into nuptial livery/physiology (phase nine, or perhaps the completion of phase eight) takes place after arrival in the ocean, but prior to mating, after which latter they die. The evolution from leptocephalus to silver eel typically takes place over a period between ten and twenty-five years—males are thought to begin silvering after about eight years in freshwater, whereas females begin the process aged fifteen. However, many live as yellow eels for much longer than this—some eels kept in captivity have lived to the ages of seventy or more. **Bright lens of brine** ... **Antarctic Bottoms** ... **North Atlantic Gyre**—the warm saline waters of the Sargasso are three feet higher in the centre of the Sea than at the edges, due to the action of the North Atlantic Gyre; the Sargasso sits on a layer of freezing water that originates in currents exiting the Weddell Sea. The five **Grumman Avengers** of Flight 19 disappeared in the Sargasso's 'Bermuda Triangle' on 5th December, 1945.

ELEVEN. The **Deep Scattering** Layer (DSL) of the Sargasso is a phenomenon detected by radar, created by the mass migration of oceanic creatures from the mesopelagic to the epipelagic in darkness (to feed) and a corresponding return migration to the mesopelagic in daylight (to avoid predators). The mass of creatures involved in this 'diel vertical migration'—plankton, small fishes, shrimp, squid, etc—is so great, it shows as an entity on radar. Leptocephali rise and fall in the DSL with the other creatures. **Phototaxic**—eels have five taxes, or migratory reflexes, which manifest in different ways at different stages of their life-cycle: *halotaxis* is reaction to water salinity—ascending eels are attracted to less saline water, descending eels to more saline water; *phototaxis* is reaction to light—eels always seek to avoid light and cleave to the darkness; *rheotaxis* is reaction to currents—broadly, ascending eels swim against the current, whilst descending they swim with it; *stereotaxis* is reaction to contact with solid bodies—eels prefer to live and travel along banks and bottoms; *thermotaxis* is reaction to heat—eels are much more active in warm water than in cold, a clue to their origin as a tropical species. It is thought that one of the ways European eels identify their breeding grounds is by the elevated water temperature. **Deepwater Horizon** was the oil-drilling rig that blew-out in the Gulf of Mexico in 2010, causing one of the biggest marine pollution events of modern times. The **Gulf Stream** is an ocean current running north along the coast of North America. At its point of maximum flow, off the Carolinas, its volume is around seventy million cubic metres per second—3,500 times greater than the flow of the Mississippi, apparently. Its velocity diminishes as it turns eastward off Cape Hatteras. Off Newfoundland it loses most of its thrust and diffuses into general North Atlantic Drift. **Oestrogen … neonicotinoid run-off** refers to the demonstrated but as yet unquantifiable potential of hormones and chemicals to interfere with eel physiology and reproductive biology. 90% of eels are hermaphrodite on hatching (the remaining 10% are born definitively female) and only become definitively male or female during their freshwater phase. It is thought that exposure to anthropogenic oestrogen in sewage outflows may result in disproportionate numbers of hermaphrodite eels becoming female, with obvious implications for breeding success.

THIRTEEN. **Panamax freighters** are the largest cargo vessels able to pass through the Panama Canal. **Atlantic's Niño** alludes to the Pacific-based current and climate phenomenon, El Niño, referring to the possible reversal of the Gulf Stream that might occur if the planet continues to warm. **Grand Banks**—the formerly rich fishing grounds off Newfoundland which saw the collapse of **cod** stocks to 1% of historic levels in 1992 (they have never really recovered) and which previously had seen the virtual extermination of the **right whale** and the actual extermination of the Great **auk**, whose last stronghold was on **Funk** Island. Newfoundland's native **Beothuk** Indians would paddle thirty miles into the Atlantic where they would take sustainable harvests of Funk's millions of nesting seabirds, including Great auks, as part of their subsistence economy. European colonists, however, camped out on the island for months and took huge quantities of birds for commercial purposes—meat, oil, eggs and feathers—they even improvised rendering plants on the island. The flightless Great auks were particularly defenceless against this onslaught, and by 1780 were extirpated from the island. After the destruction of the relict Icelandic population in 1844 (by collectors), the Great auk became totally extinct. The Beothuk themselves were extinct by 1829. The **Gaels of Uist** were forcibly deported from their homeland in the 19th century by their absentee landlord, John Gordon of Cluny. They were transported to Nova Scotia, where they were abandoned.

FOURTEEN. The **North Atlantic Drift** is the North Atlantic's dominant north-west current. Unlike the Gulf Stream, which is wind-driven, the North Atlantic Drift is **thermohaline**, that is, the direction and speed of flow is determined by surface water temperature and its salt content relative to other water masses. **Western Sahara**— the North Atlantic Drift carries some European eels to North Africa, although the vast majority arrive in European estuaries and rivers. Some European eels also find their way into Asiatic river systems via the Mediterranean and Black Seas. A **cetorhine** is a Basking Shark. Although it has long been asserted that leptocephali are **helpless drifters** on the currents, unable to swim directionally, recent evidence has confirmed that which many have long suspected, that they are capable of directional swimming to a limited extent. The meta-morphosis to **glass eel** that precedes the invasion of continental waters—**they somehow drop invisible anchors and hold / against the flow**—has been understood as implying a kind of deliberate halt. Exactly how and where it happens is yet another of the mysteries pertaining to the life cycle of *Anguilla anguilla*. **Myomeres** are the chevron-shaped blocks of muscle in leptocephali that develop into the spinal column of elvers.

SEVENTEEN. **Gadoids** are fish of the cod family. **Ívarr** the Boneless was the Viking King who led the Great Heathen Army that conquered and settled much of England. He and his army entered the country in 865 via the Humber.

NINETEEN. European eels are *euryhaline* fish, meaning that they can pass easily between salt and fresh water. They are able to do so primarily because of the **mucus** they are coated in, which mitigates osmotic pressures and helps them maintain internal isotonicity. The **toxic** blood of the European eel contains a poison named *ichthyotoxin*, which is harmful and potentially fatal to humans if introduced into the bloodstream in sufficient quantities, through an open wound, for example. It is thought that ichthyotoxin's anti-pathogenic qualities help eels to survive in the bacteria-laden waters in which they often live—the *toxic* function of the blood has a *tonic* function in relation to the health of the eel. **Three Ridings & Five Boroughs**—the Viking divisions of Yorkshire and the Mercian Danelaw: the North, West, and East Ridings of Yorkshire & Lindsey, and the Boroughs of Derby, Leicester, Lincoln, Nottingham and Stamford. These areas are drained by the eely catchments of the rivers Trent and Ouse, which join to form the Humber Estuary. **Eiríkr** Blóðøx was King of Norway & Northumbria in the mid-10th century.

TWENTY. **Hand nets**, or 'dip nets', are essentially huge versions of children's long-handled fishing nets. They are the traditional tools used in the harvesting of elvers. **Northfield's … and Moors**—in the 1970s, the three 'houses' at Northfield Middle School, South Kirkby, were named for the Tory Highlands of Yorkshire. The **Dutchman** Cornelius **Vermuyden** (1595–1677) was employed by Charles I to drain the Yorkshire Fen in the 1620s & 30s. He drained Thorne Mere, canalised the three meandering branches of the Don into the single embanked drain of the so-called 'Dutch River' and straightened and embanked several other rivers—in the process turning hundreds of square miles of fen into arable farmland, precipitating a social, cultural and environmental holocaust the scale of which we might begin to appreciate if we imagine a similar atrocity being inflicted on the Okavango or Camargue. The **Amazon Fulfilment Centre** is located between the river Torne and Yorkshire Wildlife Trust's Potteric Carr reserve. A **bootlace** is the name given by anglers to very small **yellow eels**.

TWENTY-TWO. **Ulleskelf** is a hamlet on the river Wharfe near Tadcaster. I used to fish there in the late 70s. I never caught anything other than eels—mostly bootlaces—although my mates, more expert anglers, would catch flatties, pike, dace, barbel, chub, perch, roach and ruffe. Ulleskelf was once the location of a commercial eel fishery, and although the official etymology of the name derives it from a combination of the Norse personal name *Úlfr* and *Kelf*, the Old Norse for 'calf', perhaps an origin in 'eel' (*ǣl*, Old English, *âl*, Old Norse) and the Old English *scelf/scylf* ('piece of land') makes much more sense ('Eel-Place') than the preposterous 'Ulf's Calf'. The name is given in Domesday as *Oleschel* and *Oleslec*. **Oligocene Tethys**— the ancestors of anguillid eels evolved in the Eocene and Oligocene epochs, between 30 and 50 million years ago. **Tethys** was a prehistoric ocean. **Thorpe Marsh** power station was built in 1959, on the banks of the river Don at Barnby Dun, near its confluence with the **Ea Beck**. It was closed in 1994, but the cooling towers were not demolished until 2012. **Ea** is Old English for 'river'. An **anadromous** fish is born in the river and migrates to sea, returning to the river to breed. A **redd** is the name given to a salmon's spawning scrape or to the spawning area itself. **Mindless, reliable, pot-luck currents … Tagus, Severn and Loire**—eels do not 'return' to the rivers their parents lived in, as is sometimes asserted. They are distributed to the freshwaters in which they spend their adult lives purely by chance. An elver that is the offspring of, say, a male that spent his life in an Icelandic river and a female who spent her life in an Italian lagoon, might be distributed by the currents to any landmass of the eastern North Atlantic from the Tropic of Cancer to the Arctic Circle.

TWENTY-THREE. The European eel had evolved, or a species very like it had, by the **Miocene** epoch, around five million years ago.

TWENTY-FIVE. **Dredged and piled … suffocating eels**— in 2011, when a 400 yard stretch of the river Went was deepened near Thorpe Audlin, I found over 250 dead and dying yellow eels in the heaps of silts that had been dumped bankside by the excavator. **Richard** is Richard Rolle (1300–1349), the 'Hermit of Hampole'

(Barnsdale, in the West Riding of Yorkshire). **Robin Hood's Well** was a roadside spring and associated festival ground located on the Great North Road in Barnsdale, a few hundred yards above the Ea Beck. Henry VIII held a tournament and games at the Well in the summer of 1541, on the occasion of the post-Pilgrimage of Grace submission of the Northern nobles. This 'progress' was the only time in his reign that Henry ever visited 'the North'. He made it to Pontefract and Sandal (Wakefield) castles before he got a nosebleed and turned back.

TWENTY-SIX. **Another crawling culvert**—the number of culverts (beneath roads, under railways and in built-up areas) migratory eels have to negotiate in (post) industrial Yorkshire is enormous. Because many of them have 'lips' or shallow water at entry and exit, especially during periods of low flow, eels are often delayed or obstructed as they attempt to progress, and thus become vulnerable to predation—by otters, mink, cormorants and herons—even by smaller mustelids, corvids and raptors. Eels are similarly vulnerable at weirs, sluices and when using certain types of fish pass.

TWENTY-EIGHT. **Tangle of tiny dikes and streams**—in my research for this book I trapped eels in watercourses that were no more than three feet wide and two feet deep, right at the extremity of the Went and Ea catchments. **The H&B spur** is a short, now closed-down, offshoot of the Hull & Barnsley railway that curves across South Elmsall common to the site of Frickley Colliery.

TWENTY-NINE. During the 1980s and 1990s, the Victorian stone bridges that crossed farmland streams in South/West Yorkshire, and which often held colonies of bats and nests of swallows under their arches, were left to collapse, or were replaced with **concrete pipes**. The stones of the bridges the pipes replaced were typically abandoned in the watercourses.

THIRTY-ONE. The **Landrace** is a breed of domestic pig commonly farmed in intensive units.

THIRTY-THREE. **Inexhaustible biomass**—although European eels are still found in many rivers, sometimes in what seems reasonable numbers, the calamitous speed of the collapse of their population is analogous to that of the Passenger Pigeon, which once accounted for between 25 and 40 percent of the avian biomass of the United States, and which, as late as the 1830s, existed in flocks numbering in the billions. The population began to sharply decline (due to uncontrolled hunting, commercial exploitation on their breeding grounds and deforestation) from the mid-19th century. The last mass breeding took place in 1878, at Petoskey, Michigan, where as many as 50,000 birds were slaughtered daily for a period of several months. From that point the population of the Passenger Pigeon collapsed, and by 1900 it was extinct in the wild. Although it is often asserted that eels are carrion eaters, they prefer to eat live food, and will not eat putrefying flesh or anything that has been **too long dead**. **Mijbil** was Gavin Maxwell's pet otter, **Toki** was a cheetah rescued and filmed by Simon King, and **Christian the Hugging Lion** was a lion purchased from Harrods by John Rendall and Anthony Bourke in 1969. He was later released in Africa by George Adamson of *Born Free* fame.

THIRTY-FOUR. **Nineteen inches … so conceivably a he, even from the catchment's far extremity**—female eels are larger than males (any eel over 50cm is almost certainly female and any silver eel under 40cm is almost certainly male, with yellow or silver eels in the 40cm–50cm range being either male or female). Female eels tend to penetrate farther up the catchment, whereas males are more likely to remain in estuaries and harbours.

THIRTY-FIVE. **Was she silvering?**—in the months before they begin their journey to Sargasso, European eels metamorphose into 'silver eels', the visible characteristics of which are: pelagic counter-shaded livery (blue/black above, white below, with a metallic sheen); long pectoral fins and very large eyes. **Julius foul-hooked**—because the digestive systems of silver eels are atrophied, they do not feed, although they sometimes lunge atavistically at baits. On this occasion the fish was foul-hooked, in the pectoral fin, if I remember correctly.

THIRTY-EIGHT. **Dark moon**—as eels are phototaxic, they avoid even dim light, preferring to begin their migration in the pitch-dark of the New Moon. **Slick with gleaming fat**—the silver eel is the gourmet's eel.

THIRTY-NINE. **Abandons her length to the current**—silver eels seem to migrate passively when possible, probably as an energy saving device, allowing themselves to be taken by the current or tide. In conditions of spate, this mode of travel can be very rapid.

FORTY-ONE. Silver eels are commercially harvested by means of **fyke or wing nets**. The blades of **Archimedes Screw** and other hydro-electric plant (HEP) turbines (for example, at the Ardnacrusha HEP on Ireland's river Shannon and the *eight* HEPs on Sweden's river Atran) kill and maim millions of migrating silver eels every year. **Trent Falls**—the confluence of the rivers Ouse and Trent between Faxfleet in Yorkshire and Alkborough in Lincolnshire. **Catadromous**—a fish that is born at sea, migrates to freshwater to live out the majority of its life-cycle, and returns to the sea to breed.

FORTY-TWO. **Procellariiform**—'tube-nosed', the name given to birds of the petrel and albatross families because of the peculiar tube-like form of their nostrils. The eel's nostrils also take the form of external tubes. **Imprinted geomagnetic memory**—elvers imprint the details of estuarine tidal currents in their brains, as a navigational aid. **Benthic**—pertaining to the bed or bottom of any body of water. European **sturgeon** were found in the rivers of the Humber catchment in ever-diminishing numbers throughout the modern period and well into the twentieth century. Sturgeon are extremely long-lived fish (up to and beyond 100 years) and with age they can become huge— records indicate that some captured individuals exceeded fifteen feet in length and it is thought that some individuals may have reached twenty feet or even longer. Now on the verge of extinction, the only wild population, a maximum of 800 individuals, and probably far fewer, exists in the Gironde river system in south-west France. A captive breeding programme (they have not bred in the wild in their native rivers since 1994 because HEPs and other dams prevent them from migrating upriver to their redds) has enabled some limited reintroductions into the Dordogne, Garonne, the Dutch Rhine and the German Elbe and Oder. Sturgeon do not become sexually mature until they are ten or fifteen years old, so the outcomes of these reintroductions will not be known for decades. **Donna Nook** is an RAF base on the coast of North Lincolnshire where **Thunderbolt** attack aircraft test their weaponry on an offshore bombing range.

FORTY-FOUR. The *Anguillicola* **nematode** (*Anguillicola crassus*) is a parasite that infests the swim bladders of eels, affecting their ability to control their buoyancy. The nematode also weakens their immune systems and causes other physiological problems. It is thought to be a factor in the decline of European eels. *Anguillicola crassus* was inadvertently imported to Europe from Eastern Asia in the swim bladders of imported ornamental fish. **Benzoylecgonine** is a metabolite of cocaine found in the tissues of eels in the Thames catchment and in other rivers that flow through cities where the recreational use of cocaine is endemic. It causes hyperactivity, nervous disorders and ultimately death in eels.

FORTY-FIVE. Although silver eels are easily netted in rivers, very few have been caught at sea. Consequently, we know virtually nothing about their migration after they leave their rivers. A few European silver eels have been caught as **accidentals** by fishermen in the Mediterranean and in the English Channel. One was caught off the Hebrides, in the stomach of a long-lined Mora (**googly-eyed cod**); others have been found off Ireland in the guts of scabbardfish; one was found in the stomach of a sperm whale (**cachalot**) killed off the Azores by the Prince of Monaco. Fish tagged with data-loggers released in the Atlantic off France and Ireland travelled at depths between 300 and 800 metres, where three of them were predated by toothed whales. The wreck of HMS **Affray** lies at the bottom of the English Channel, as does the **Piper Malibu** the Argentinian football player Emiliano **Sala** was travelling in when it crashed in January, 2019. **No synchronous … fish**—the little evidence we have seems to suggest that European eels migrate at great depths in the mesopelagic, across vast areas of ocean. Accordingly, eels are unlikely to form dense shoals, even though tens or hundreds of millions may be travelling at any given time.

FORTY-SEVEN. **Xiphius, macrocephalus … architeuthis**—swordfish, sperm whales and giant squids, respectively.

FORTY-EIGHT. **Entorhinal**—the cortex entorhinalis is the part of the brain concerned with memory and navigation. **Fifteen, twenty … twenty-five miles a day**—the precise route the European eel takes to the Sargasso is unknown, as is the speed at which it travels. For the purposes of the poem I assume eels travel on the currents of the North Atlantic Gyre, picking up the circulation with the Azores Current. The speed of currents of the Gyre is highly variable, but would allow efficient, semi-passive travel within the range of the speeds given in the poem. **Seawolves** are U.S. nuclear submarines.

FIFTY. **The cordon narrows ... deep-spaced shoal**—I imagine the migratory eels beginning to travel in closer proximity as they close in on Sargasso, using scent to find each other prior to breeding. **Three or four million eggs**—only Atlantic Cod (*Gadus morhua*) rival the European eel in terms of the sheer quantity of ova produced by a single female. **Recycling**—as eels get closer to Sargasso, their migration, or pelagic, livery almost certainly begins to change into breeding livery. To effect this transformation, the metamorphosis eels are already undergoing intensifies, redirecting minerals and other resources from their bones, digestive systems and eyes into their reproductive organs, resulting in their bodies becoming floppy, rubberised and waterlogged. At the point of mating they are already on the verge of death. **Eight months and six thousand fasting miles**—the distance eels travel on their migrations and how long it takes them are disputed, with some recent research suggesting eels may take over a year to make their catadromous migration.

FIFTY-ONE. **Imprinted larval hippocampus**—the part of the brain in which the elver stores its magnetic memory map to Sargasso. **Heat and salinity fronts**—the eel's thermo- and halo- taxes help them recognise the warm, salty water of their breeding grounds. **Fifteen-hundred feet**—the evidence, such as it is, suggests that migratory eels travel at around this depth. **Photocline**—a coinage on the model of thermocline, the boundary between the epipelagic and the mesopelagic.

FIFTY-THREE. **Completes ... the reprogramming of her body**—eels do not eat for the duration of the migration. They derive energy from body fat and by metabolising their skeletons, digestive systems and other body parts.

FIFTY-FOUR. **Blood red speckling ... upstream salmon**—male European eels artificially brought to sexual maturity by hormone injections take on the livery described. **Fourteen-inch veterans [...] females, girthy as pythons, four or five feet long**—while some male eels that set off to Sargasso are tiny, some of the females are very large indeed, including individuals of fifteen pounds or more. The largest European eel reliably recorded was caught in the Orlik reservoir in the Czech Republic in 1987, and weighed fifteen pounds and seven ounces. Several unverified—but not necessarily unreliable—

claims refer to individuals over six feet in length and weighing up to thirty pounds. The current British record is an 11lb 2oz fish, caught by Steve Terry, at Kingfisher Lake in Hampshire, in 1978. However, in July 2019, a 'potential record' eel was captured on the River Thames at Richmond, in an electrofishing survey conducted by the Environment Agency. The eel was measured at four-and-a-half feet in length, but was not weighed. Standard length/weight conversion techniques give its weight as 12lb 10oz.

FIFTY-SIX. **Dead and dying eels**—it is believed that European eels die after mating and spawning, a supposition confirmed by the fact that all captive European eels that have been artificially brought to sexual maturity in aquaria have died within hours of ejaculation/spawning. A forty-year-old female eel kept in the Maretarium aquarium at Kotka, Finland, 'spontaneously matured' in 2019, and died with a coelum packed with ripe eggs.

FIFTY-SEVEN. **Red clays**—the seabed of the Sargasso is made up of a fine sediment called 'red clay'—at least partly comprised, one imagines, of the remains of incalculable numbers of dead eels. **He stiffens … hokey-cokey**—the breeding livery and mating ritual of European eels has never been observed in the wild and the description here is based on laboratory descriptions, the livery and ritual of the closely related Pacific/Indian Ocean species *Anguilla japonica* (the Japanese eel) and *Anguilla marmorata* (the Giant mottled eel)—and imagination. Despite the monogamous ritual described in the poem, it is thought that both female and male anguillid eels can, and do, breed with multiple partners before they spend themselves and die.

FIFTY-NINE. **Archaea** is the name given to the epoch of geological time stretching from 2.5 to 4.0 million years ago, in which period life evolved on Earth. **Pleroma**—the fullness of life and spirit on Earth, symbolised as a single flame.

Select Bibliography

Aarestrup, K. et al. (2008). 'Survival and behaviour of European silver eel in late freshwater and early marine phase during spring migration'. *Fisheries Management and Ecology*, Vol. 15 (5–6), 435–440.

Aarestrup, K. et al. (2009). 'Oceanic Spawning Migration of the European Eel (*Anguilla anguilla*)'. *Science*, Vol. 325 (5948), 1660. Washington, D.C.: AAAS.

Aida, K. et al. (2003). *Eel Biology*. Dordrecht: Springer.

Andrews, E. (2020). 'The Mysterious Disappearance of Flight 19'. *History.com*, 1 September 2020. https://www.history.com/news/the-mysterious-disappearance-of-flight-19. Retrieved 26 March 2020.

Aphramian, M. & Walker, A. (2009). 'Status of eel fisheries, stocks and their management in England and Wales'. *Knowledge & Management of Aquatic Ecosystems*, No. 390–91, Art. 07. https://doi.org/10.1051/kmae/2009007. Retrieved 26 March 2020.

Ayala, D. J. & Munk, P. (2018). 'Growth rate variability of larval European eels (*Anguilla anguilla*) across the extensive eel spawning area in the southern Sargasso Sea'. *Fisheries Oceanography*, Vol. 27 (6), 525–535.

Barry, J. et al. (2016). 'Freshwater and coastal migration patterns in the silver-stage eel Anguilla anguilla'. *Journal of Fish Biology*, Vol. 88 (2), 676–689.

Berann, H. (1977). 'Atlantic Ocean Floor'. *ICA Commission on Map Design*. https://mapdesign.icaci.org/map-examples/. Retrieved 26 March 2020.

Bertin, L. (1956). *Eels: A Biological Study*. London: Cleaver-Hume Press.

Bischoff, B. et al. (N.D.). 'The North Atlantic Drift Current'. *Ocean Surface Currents*. https://oceancurrents.rsmas.miami.edu/atlantic/north-atlantic-drift.html. Retrieved 26 March 2020.

Boëtius, I. & Boëtius, J. (1980). 'Experimental maturation of female silver eels, *Anguilla anguilla*. Estimates of fecundity and energy reserves for migration and spawning'. *Dana*, Vol. 1, 1–28.

Bunting, W. et al. (1974). 'The History and Distribution of Fish in the Doncaster District'. *The Naturalist* 929, 41–55. York: Yorkshire Naturalists' Union.

Byford, D. (2005). *Agricultural Change in the Lowlands of South Yorkshire with Special Reference to the Manor of Hatfield, 1600–c.1875*. Unpublished Ph.D thesis, University of Sheffield.

Calles, O. et al. (2010). 'Size-dependent mortality of migratory silver eels at a hydropower plant, and implications for escapement to the sea'. *Freshwater Biology*, Vol. 55 (10), 2167–2180.

Capaldo, E. et al. (2018). 'Effects of environmental cocaine concentrations on the skeletal muscle of the European eel (*Anguilla anguilla*)'. *Science of the Total Environment*, Vol. 640–641, 862-873.

Caufield, C. & Godwin, F. (1991). *Thorne Moors*. St. Albans: Sumach Press.

Crawford, B. (1975). *Catch More Eels*. London: Wolfe Publishing.

Cresci, A. et al. (2019). 'Glass eels (*Anguilla anguilla*) imprint the magnetic direction of tidal currents from their juvenile estuaries'. *Communications Biology*, No. 2, Art. 366.

de Menezes, J. (2020). 'Emiliano Sala crash: Pilot David Ibbotson was not cleared to fly plane, report finds'. *The Independent*, 13 03 2020. https://www.independentco.uk/sport/football/news/emiliano-sala-crash-pilot-report-david-ibbotson-death-nantes-cardiff-a9400286.html. Retrieved 26 March 2020.

Dekker, W. (2003). 'Did lack of spawners cause the collapse of the European eel, *Anguilla anguilla*?' *Fisheries Management and Ecology*, Vol. 10 (6), 365–376.

Devine, T. M. (2019). *The Scottish Clearances: A History of the Dispossessed*. London: Penguin.

Doble, C. et al. (2015). *The River Thames European Eel Monitoring Project Report, 2011–2014*. London: ZSL.

Environment Agency. (N.D.). *Elver & Eel Passes: A guide to the design and implementation of passage solutions at weirs, tidal gates and sluices*. Bristol: Environment Agency. https://assets.publishing.service.gov.uk/government/uploads/system/uploads/attachment_data/file/297338/geho0411btqc-e-e.pdf. Retrieved 26 March 2020.

The European Space Agency. (N.D.). 'The North Atlantic Gyre'. https://www.esa.int/SPECIALS/Eduspace_Weather_EN/SEM1H-YK1YHH_0.html. Retrieved 26 March 2020.

Feunteun, E. (2002). 'Management and restoration of European eel population (*Anguilla anguilla*): An impossible bargain'. *Ecological Engineering*, Vol. 18 (5), 575–591.

Fort, T. (2002). *The Book of Eels: On the Trail of the Thin-heads*. London: HarperCollins Publishers.

Freese, M. et al. (2009). 'Bone resorption and body reorganization during maturation induce maternal transfer of toxic metals in anguillid eels'. *Proceedings of the National Academy of Sciences of the United States of America*, Vol. 116 (23), 11339–11344.

Fricke, H. (1995). 'Tracking of artificially matured eels (*Anguilla anguilla*) in the Sargasso Sea and the problem of the eel's spawning site'. *Naturwissenschaften*, Vol. 82 (1), 32–36.

Fuglister, F. C. (1954). 'Average Temperature and Salinity at a Depth of 200 Meters in the North Atlantic'. *Tellus*, Vol. 6 (1), 46–58.

Fuller, E. (1999). *The Great Auk*. Southborough: Errol Fuller.

Fuller, E. (2000). *Extinct Birds*. Oxford: Oxford University Press.

GEBCO Undersea Features Gazetteer (N.D.). https://www.ngdc.noaa.gov/gazetteer/. Retrieved 26 March 2020.

Geßner, J. et al. (2010). *German Action Plan for the conservation and restoration of the European Sturgeon (Acipenser sturio)*. Bonn: Federal Ministry for the Environment, Nature Conservation and Nuclear Safety (BMU).

Gollock, M. et al. (2019). *Status of non-CITES listed anguillid eels*. London: ZSL.

Heuvelmans, B. (1968). *In the Wake of the Sea-Serpents*. London: Rupert Hart-Davis.

Houben, B. and Blom, E. (2015). 'The Rhine Sturgeon Project: A Brief Overview and a Look into the Future'. *International Conference on Engineering and Ecohydrology for Fish Passage*. ScholarWorks@UMass Amherst.

Jacobs, F. & Gourley, J. (1973). *The Freshwater Eel*. Kingswood: The Windmill Press.

Jacoby, D. M. P. et al. (2015). 'Synergistic patterns of threat and the challenges facing global anguillid eel conservation'. *Global Ecology and Conservation*, Vol. 4, 321–333.

Jacoby, D. & Gollock, M. (2014). *Anguilla anguilla. The IUCN Red List of Threatened Species 2014.* Gland, Switzerland: IUCN.

Liu, W. et al. (2017). 'Overlooked possibility of a collapsed Atlantic Meridional Overturning Circulation in warming climate'. *Science Advances*, Vol. 3 (1), 1–7.

Locker, A. (2018). *Freshwater Fish in England.* Oxford: Oxbow Books.

Magri MacMahon, A. F. (1946). *Fishlore.* Harmondsworth: Pelican.

Manville Fenn, G. (1906). *Dick O' the Fens.* London: Blackie & Son.

Mason, B. (2017). 'How One Brilliant Woman Mapped the Ocean Floor's Secrets'. https://www.nationalgeographic.com/news/2017/02/marie-tharp-map-ocean-floor/. Retrieved 26 March 2020.

Miller, M. J. (2009). 'Ecology of Anguilliform Leptocephali: Remarkable Transparent Fish Larvae of the Ocean Surface Layer'. *Aqua-BioScience Monographs*, Vol. 2 (4), 1–94.

Miller, M. J. et al. (2019). 'Spawning by the European eel across 2000km of the Sargasso Sea'. *Biology Letters*, Vol. 15 (4), 1–5.

Moriarty, C. (1978). *Eels: A Natural and Unnatural History.* Newton Abbott: David & Charles.

Musing, L. et al. (2018). *Implementation of the CITES Appendix II listing of European Eel* Anguillla anguilla. *Annex 1.* London: Zoological Society of London / Traffic.

National Weather Service. (N.D.). 'Layers of the Ocean'. https://www.weather.gov/jetstream/layers_ocean. Retrieved 26 March 2020.

Nunn, A. D. et al. (2007). *Humber eel management issues: barriers and stocking. Final Report.* Hull: University of Hull International Fisheries Institute.

Pallardy, R. (2020). 'Deepwater Horizon oil spill', *Brittanica.com.* 13 03 2020. https://www.britannica.com/event/Deepwater-Horizon-oil-spill. Retrieved 26 March 2020.

Pastore, R. T. (1997). 'The Boethuk', heritage.nf.ca. https://www.heritage.nf.ca/articles/aboriginal/beothuk.php. Retrieved 26 March 2020.

Perrett, R. (1958). *Eels: How to Catch Them.* London: Herbert Jenkins.

Piper, A. T. et al. (2018). 'The impact of an Archimedes Screw hydropower turbine on fish migration in a lowland river'. *Ecological Engineering*, Vol. 118, 31–42.

Prosek, J. (2010). *Eels*. New York: HarperCollins Publishers.

'Record Eel Discovered'. (1 July 2019). https://www.anglingtimes. co.uk/news-2019/potential-record-eel-discovered. Retrieved 25 March 2020.

Righton, D. et al. (2012). 'The *Anguilla* spp. migration problem: 40 million years of evolution and two millennia of speculation'. *Journal of Fish Biology*, Vol. 81 (2), 365–386.

Righton, D. et al. (2016). 'Empirical observations of the spawning migration of European eels: The long and dangerous road to the Sargasso Sea'. *Science Advances*, Vol. 2 (10), 1–14.

Rolvien, T. et al. (2016). 'How the European eel (*Anguilla anguilla*) loses its skeletal framework across lifetime'. *Proceedings of the Royal Society B*, Vol. 283 (1841), 1–10.

Rotherham, I. D. (2010). *Yorkshire's Forgotten Fenlands*. Barnsley: Wharncliffe.

Sánchez-Guillamón, O. et al. (2018). 'Shape and Size Complexity of Deep Seafloor Mounds on the Canary Basin (West to Canary Islands, Eastern Atlantic): A DEM-Based Geomorphometric Analysis of Domes and Volcanoes'. *Geosciences* 2018, Vol. 8 (2), No. 37, 1–22.

Schweid, R. (2009). *Consider the Eel*. Cambridge, Ma: Da Capo.

Schweid, R. (2009). *Eel*. London: Reaktion Books.

Teal, M. & Teal, J. (1975). *The Sargasso Sea*. Boston: Little, Brown and Company.

Terech-Majewska, E. et al. (2015). 'Influence of nematode *Anguillicoloides crassus* infestation on the cellular and humoral innate immunity in European eel (*Anguilla anguilla* L.)'. *Central European Journal of Immunology*, Vol. 40 (2), 127–131.

Tesch, F. W. (1977). *The Eel: Biology and Management of Anguillid Eels*. London: Chapman and Hall.

Thornton, T. (2009). 'Henry VIII's Progress Through Yorkshire in 1541 and its Implications for Northern Identities'. *Northern History*, Vol. 46 (2), 231–244.

Tsukamoto, K. (2006). 'Spawning of eels near a seamount'. *Nature*, Vol. 439, 929. https://doi.org/10.1038/439929a. Retrieved 26 March 2020.

Tsukamoto, K. et al. (2011). 'Oceanic spawning ecology of freshwater eels in the western North Pacific'. *Nature Communications* 2, Art. 179. https://doi.org/10.1038/ncomms1174. Retrieved 26 March 2020.

von Ginneken, V. J. T. and Maes, G. E. (2005). 'The European eel (*Anguilla anguilla*, Linnaeus), its Lifecycle, Evolution and Reproduction: A Literature Review'. *Reviews in Fish Biology and Fisheries*, Vol. 15 (4), 367–398.

Wageningen University and Research. (2019). 'First observation ever of a spontaneously matured female European eel', https://www.wur.nl/en/Research-Results/Research-Institutes/livestock-research/show-wlr/First-observation-ever-of-a-spontaneously-matured-female-European-eel.htm. Retrieved 26 March 2020.

Wahlberg, M. et al. (2014). 'Evidence of marine mammal predation of the European eel (*Anguilla anguilla* L.) on its marine migration'. *Deep Sea Research Part I: Oceanographic Research Papers*, Vol. 86, 32–38.

Wood, R. (2011). 'Tethys Ocean'. *Encyclopedia of Modern Coral Reefs*. Dordrecht: Springer. https:/link.springer.com/referencework-entry/10.1007%2F978-90-481-2639-2_158. Retrieved 26 March 2020.

Wyatt-Greenlee, R. (N.D.). 'Eel-Rents Project'. *Historia Cartarum*. http://historiacartarum.org/eel-rents-project/. Retrieved 26 March 2020.

Zoological Society of London. (2017). *The Thames European Eel Project Report, 2017*. London: ZSL.

Zoological Society of London. (2018). *The Thames European Eel Project Report, 2018*. London: ZSL.

Acknowledgements

The expertise, advice and support of the following people was invaluable to the development of *The European Eel*: Dr Matthew Gollock, Marine and Freshwater Programme Manager at the Zoological Society of London and Chair of the Anguillid Eel Specialist Group; Bram Houben, Ecologist/Wildlife Biologist at ARK Natuurontwikkeling, Netherlands; Paul Kemp, Professor of Ecological Engineering at the Faculty of Engineering and Physical Sciences, University of Southampton; and Pete Wall, Dearne Valley Living Landscape Manager with the Yorkshire Wildlife Trust.

Special thanks are due to P. R. Ruby for her striking and evocative artwork and her wider contributions to the collaboration, and to Brian Lewis of Longbarrow Press for his steadfast support of this unlikely project, and for the care, creativity and determination he showed in bringing it to fruition.

Finally, thanks to the University of Huddersfield for the small research grant that enabled some eel-related travel and some unusual literary kit: chest waders, kick nets, eel-traps and an aquarium.